Mind, Body, Spirit
Connecting With Your Creative Self

Mary T. Braheny and
Diane S. Halperin

Health Communications, Inc.
Deerfield Beach, Florida

Library of Congress Cataloging-in-Publication Data

Braheny, Mary T.
    Mind, Body, Spirit: connecting with your creative self / by
Mary T. Braheny, Diane S. Halperin.
        p.   cm.
    ISBN 1-55874-039-2
    1. Arts — Therapeutic use.   2. Co-dependence (Psychology)
— Treatment.   I. Halperin, Diane S., 1946—   II. Title.
    RC489.A72B73   1989   89-11152
    615.8'515—dc20   CIP

© 1989 Mary T. Braheny and Diane S. Halperin

ISBN 1-55874-039-2

Publisher: Health Communications, Inc.
            3201 S.W. 15th Street
            Deerfield Beach, Florida 33442

Cover design by Reta Thomas

ACKNOWLEDGMENTS

There are many people to thank for supporting our vision, among them . . .

Barry, Cec, Yale, Ida — our parents — for their ideals, nourishment and the tools to be creative

Howard, Ronna, John, Dan, Kevin — our brothers and sister — for inspiration, constant support and for being great playmates

Rokelle Lerner for her encouragement and the ability to open doors

Barb Naiditch for spreading our work to the four corners

Gary Seidler and Peter Vegso for investing their Mind, Body, Spirit

Our clients for teaching us to be creative arts therapists

Our friends for their creative talents and loving wisdom

DEDICATION

To those souls — past, present and future
                           who choose to live their lives as an art form

CONTENTS

PREFACE

We're living in the Era of the Written Word with access to worlds of information. Our task is to glean the wisdom from these worlds of data.

One of the ageless ways of acquiring wisdom is through the process of listening to our unknown Self and using its wisdom in everyday life. In crisis, conflict, chaos, our ally is our *creative* use of information to resolve issues wisely. Thus, the exploration and frequent experience of the creative arts encourages the *living* of our potentials.

As creative arts therapists, our task has been to give innovative forms to linear information. Entering the mental health field, a highly cognitive profession, has encouraged the dialogue between verbal and nonverbal therapy, the rational and intuitive, the medical model and creative expression.

Our creativity has been stretched through our work with a wide variety of populations. We have brought the creative arts to autistic toddlers, the educationally handicapped, psychotic and acting-out adolescents, substance abusers, adult children from dysfunctional families and healthy human beings seeking personal growth, as well as those resolving professional issues. Whether the crisis be the belligerent adolescent's personal issue or the professional's dilemma with a management problem, the creative process is the common denominator for these situations.

We have the privilege of witnessing and facilitating the transformative power of the creative arts. Appreciation of the creative comes not by observation alone but from observation, participation and a sense of play.

On this note, we grant you an "E" ticket to Mind, Body, Spirit.

"E" Ticket: The most exhilarating, exciting, adventurous rides in Disneyland.

INTRODUCTION AND OVERVIEW

Each person is a unity — an open system that is constantly changing. Mind, body, spirit is constantly evolving. Each part interpenetrates the others and affects the whole.

The importance of the mind, body, spirit connection is contained in the beauty and effectiveness of its functioning and expression when all is in balance. When all three aspects are clear and balanced, the interplay between them allows for magical expression in the world.

The Olympian athletes accomplish seemingly impossible feats when their minds are directing their bodies and the spirit is totally engaged. They express an ease and grace about very mindful, calculating moves. As observers, we may have felt momentarily that we were participating or believed for a second that the movements were effortless.

The power that is expressed by a balanced mind, body, spirit is often felt and recognized on a subconscious level but may not be easily talked about or named. It may be seen in an exceptional athlete who moves us, a speaker whose charismatic manner inspires us to new levels of awareness, a person who produces tremendous amounts of work seemingly effortlessly or perhaps someone who, by his or her nature, moves us in some way.

When any one of the vital three are out of alignment, we have a more difficult time staying balanced with our emotions, our clear thinking, our involvement in the world. Our lives become marked with inertia, indecision, anxieties, illness, ineffectiveness. And yet, the more in balance we are with ourselves, the less effort is needed to meet our goals, the more joy we have to share in relationships.

Spirit Needs Nourishment. Mind Needs Focus. Body Needs Direction.

It takes time to receive heart messages that nourish the spirit. Time and listening are the gestation cycle that allow the unconscious to birth our newness. The creative arts are the playground for recognizing and understanding our purpose in being here. When we truly allow our spirits to be filled with the purpose, our minds can begin to take stock of the necessary steps and needed materials so the body can become the mover or manifestor of the desire.

Sometimes in the course of our lives, we encounter obstacles that challenge our perspective and offer the opportunity to *remember* our wholeness. Growing up in an alcoholic family colors the child's perception of wholeness. The system seems closed, with little exchange within the family or from the outside world. Life is often experienced as chaotic, random, lacking consistency and follow-through. Each part of the family — each individual — has little knowledge about the other parts and how he or she affects the totality. The child's family experience becomes his world view, his way of structuring the world.

Unless there is intervention, each family member grows up to live the painful, rigid, isolated, black-and-white existence he lived as a child. Color is missing from the alcoholic family system. Color equals life, spontaneity, intimacy, exchange, people-centered versus alcoholic-centered living.

The creative arts can bring color back into a dysfunctional family and reinforce the life of each person who dares to enter the process of transformation.

The Creative Arts As Attitude, Discipline, Commitment

This book is organized in such a way as to give information about the creative arts as a self-help tool. It is designed as an experiential guide for personal growth and transformation as well as the resolution of developmental issues. It will promote your personal growth in wellness and in crisis and enhance your professional skills as a facilitator for the growth of others.

This is also a self-help manual for the resolution of conflicts arising in dysfunctional families. Although families are dysfunctional for different reasons, the family patterns that evolve are similar. In the course of our work, we've used the creative arts with people whose dysfunctions arise from obstacles to growth: chemical dependency/alcoholism, eating disorders and psychosis. For the purpose of this book, we are using our work with adult children of alcoholics (ACoAs) as the focal point for our exploration in the creative arts.

The beginning of the book specifically discusses the adult child's blocks to growth and how those blocks were established on preverbal and nonverbal levels. Therefore, we look to therapies that address the issues as such. Art, movement, visualization, physical awareness and affirmation address ACoAs where they live. These modalities allow for the release of past painful conflicts and encourage and promote the vision and actualization of new potential.

We focus on and stress the importance of mind, body, spirit and the creative arts that address all three aspects of the self in order to effect a more complete transformation. In the transformational exercise section, we have included:

- **physical releases** to prepare the body for exploration
- **art** to facilitate and integrate the known and unknown pictures of the self
- **movement** to explore and practice our patterns of effectiveness in the world
- **visualization** to see our desires clearly and provide a blueprint for our direction

- **affirmation** to serve as a mental reminder of a new attitude.

The more we engage the physical, mental, emotional and spiritual parts of ourselves, the more powerful our change will be. We encourage you to participate in all the exercises.

We have used the creative arts with the developmental stages because of their importance in our continuing development. We use Eric Erikson's theory of development because it provides a flexible structure to view growth. These are some working assumptions about developmental stages and the issues that arise during each stage:

- Issues start in childhood and are recycled during our lifetime, e.g., trust in new relationships and autonomy in new jobs.
- Each stage of development is dependent upon the successful completion of the previous stage and has an effect on the body and its muscular functioning.

Each stage of development has an exercise from the modalities that address those issues.

Our hope is that this book will be a companion on your journey toward wholeness. We encourage your commitment of time, energy, space and focus in your personal development, just as you would commit to your business, family and friends. We affirm for you in this venture the attitude of love, patience and acceptance.

The exercises and physical releases described in this book are intended to promote emotional and physical integration and to provide a *gentle* means for the body to release muscular armoring. They should not be done strenuously and should not be done at all WITHOUT THE SPECIFIC APPROVAL OF YOUR PHYSICIAN. WE URGE YOU TO CONSULT WITH YOUR MEDICAL CAREGIVER BEFORE STARTING AND TO FOLLOW THE ADVICE GIVEN. If you have any physical condition which precludes doing these exercises, omit them and do all of the other art work, visualization and affirmation. You will benefit from these.

1

ACoA BLOCKS

Each of us is born into a home with particular assets and liabilities. Every parent communicates what he knows, as well as what he doesn't know. We believe that most parents do not intentionally hurt their children. Parents do the best they can with the information they have; however, their shortcomings have a tremendous effect on their children. These shortcomings, blind spots or blocks are presented and become the cutting edge of our growing and maturing.

The initial themes presented during our developing years — trust, autonomy, initiative, industry, identity — will continue to be played and replayed. Life is a constant rehearsal *and* the real performance. The liabilities can be transformed into assets in a process like the transformation of caterpillar into butterfly. The cocoon/internal transforming will continue whether we make it hard work or a learning process. Feelings will accompany the process and signal us when an old pattern is emerging. The experiencing can be lived through the desire to be a more open and expressive instrument. A block is one of life's gifts in offering the opportunity to change. We'll look at some roadblocks that impede the growth of ACoAs.

Growing up in a home where substances were abused, ACoAs lack a consistent structure. If the focus is on the substance abuser, the child often does not receive the attention he needs to feel welcome and comfortable in this world. His needs are met in a haphazard manner, on an agenda that can fluctuate between being ironclad and chaotic.

A clear sense of self and a positive regard for that emerging self doesn't happen in a substance-abusing household. The attention is on the abuser and his rollercoaster patterns. The child grows up with *holes* in his self-knowledge and self-appreciation. He may have a sense that something is missing but not be able to articulate what this means. Since many of these holes were communicated on a nonverbal level, then merely talking about what's missing will not help to experience these holes differently. Nonverbal, creative measures are needed to allow the child to experience wholeness.

Let's look at some family nonverbal patterns that can either reinforce or negate self-esteem.

Rituals

Many families have rituals — events or occasions that are set apart as special, unique to that particular family. The ritual might be a family outing, a special meal, a specific event that commemorates the beginning, ending or rite of passage for a family member or the family as a whole. These rituals help to ground, to reinforce important memories of growing up.

Many ACoAs lack family rituals. They have lived in a family structure that is chaotic, random and lacking follow-through. They have had the constant disappointment of broken promises. Often, ACoAs can't remember large portions of their childhood because pain and disappointment predominate, feelings that block memories of other childhood experiences.

As part of the healing process, ACoAs need to create rituals that mark a new way of being in life, that ground and reinforce change and create meaningful memories of joy and significance. For example, one ACoA wanted to be a dancer, dreamed of having recitals where her parents and brothers and sisters would come to witness her joy in performing. She didn't have the confidence to enroll in a dance class as a child. She was scared that her father wouldn't be sober for her recitals, that he would come drunk and embarrass her. She dreamed of being a dancer and practiced those dreams by herself but didn't dare to live them out in the larger world.

As she became active in ACoA groups and participated in therapy, she decided to take modern expressive dance classes. After six months, this young woman staged a recital at her home, complete with costumes, lighting and music. She invited her close friends to come and witness and share in her enjoyment of performance. This re-enactment of a childhood dream brought a sense of completion and marked a new beginning that reinforced living out other dreams.

Intimacy

Intimacy is another stumbling block for ACoAs. Intimacy suggests that an individual has a clear sense of boundaries; can stand on his own two feet; feels enough personal integration to meld with another and feel with another, without usurping the other's feelings; can exchange without losing a sense of self. Often in homes where substances were abused, the child has no clear modeling of intimacy. He or she might experience his parents as being abusive with each other or enmeshed or isolated or dependent — but intimacy is not known.

Since children imitate the behavior they see, siblings from dysfunctional families will imitate the same abusive, chaotic behavior with each other. Rivalry, overprotectiveness, isolation from each other and sarcasm might be the primary patterns of interaction among brothers and sisters. Often, when you obtain a family history from each sibling in an alcoholic family, the histories sound like very different families — especially depending upon whether a child is born before or after the parents' active substance abuse began.

Play

ACoAs lack family play time. Family play time offers an opportunity for members to be with each other in a spontaneous, role-free space. Play helps establish a healthy family intimacy.

But play, in the alcoholic home, is usually seen as a waste of time, something silly and frivolous, permitted only after work is done. The alcoholic parent has difficulty distinguishing between impulsiveness and playfulness. The child is too busy being a responsible little adult, a super-achiever, a clown or any of the other roles of the adult child described in Claudia Black's book, *It Will Never Happen To Me* (M.A.C., 1982). Play is soon equated with being vulnerable; vulnerability, in an alcoholic family, is synonymous with expecting to be attacked.

Vulnerability

Perhaps we look at vulnerability in terms of the *openness to attack* that the word suggests. Maybe we should look at the word as meaning *available* — that which can be had or is reachable. Many ACoAs fear or dread their vulnerability. Since fear arises whenever an ACoA feels vulnerable, we have to recontextualize the meaning in order to bring a new openness to the word. If we are not available, then there is no place to play, meet or encounter another person or the world. Being open takes practice, especially if *open* has come to mean *vulnerable*. Being open necessitates letting go of always having to control. Letting go necessitates trusting. Trusting, like anything else in life, can be practiced. When a core issue is trust then we can practice in small increments to build up a space or tolerance for trust and safety.

Responsibility

Low self-esteem sets us up for becoming over-responsible adults, another ACoA obstacle. Living in an alcoholic home we assumed, as children, that our parents' drinking was our fault. Then we began the long litany of *if only* — if only I were smarter, stronger, prettier, more lovable — then life would be different. As adults, we have to dare to update our picture of ourselves. We have to define what is in the realm of our responsibility and what belongs to someone else, and when to draw the line as to what we can do. *Wrong* often falls in the category of black-and-white thinking. Making mistakes is part of the learning process and part of being a human being.

If we can feel comfortable with the discomfort in our lives and see it as a message that we need to grow, then a block becomes an opportunity for a higher, easier level of functioning. A change of perspective provides a new set of alternatives.

2

PREMISES

Much work in the substance abuse field is focused on the integration of adult and child — the rational with the intuitive. Whether the substance is alcohol, drugs or food is secondary; the patterns that evolve from substance abuse affect families and children in similar ways. The realization that the child in us never goes away but can be highly unactualized or under-nourished has brought into focus the need for accessing that child in us. Let's look briefly at how a child develops and how that development is affected by parental substance abuse.

Our concern for the child growing up in a substance-abusing family is not for his physical well-being, except with physically abusive parents, but for how he makes sense of the actions and events occurring in his family. The child's task is to understand how to operate in the world by acting and interacting within the family. He absorbs an awareness of himself and how to survive through a world of pictures and tactile/kinesthetic impressions. Lacking sophisticated com-munication skills to check out the meaning of situations or behaviors, the child relies on his own interpretation of the events. These interpretations based on family experience are the core of his self-image and become the foundation for his functioning in the world.

A substance-abusing family, like any family, is attempting to provide the necessities of life. However, the alcoholic home environment is characterized by inconsistency and fear, guilt and blame, anger and resentment, secrecy and denial. The family focus is moved from the developmental tasks of the child to the drinking of the alcoholic parent. Childlike qualities of spontaneity, awe, curiosity, experimentation and joy are replaced by responsibility, rationality, rules, coping and seriousness.

The inconsistent interactional patterns created by focusing on the substance abuser encourages the child's use of the maladaptive coping skills of:

- **lying** to protect harmony or status quo
- **overachievement and high standards** or **low achievement and low standards** as an attempt to impact the substance abuser
- **aloofness, shyness, busyness** to avoid the parent's mixed messages about intimacy.

All this takes place in a predominantly nonverbal way and not on a conscious level. Therefore the patterns go very deep for the child of a substance abuser. Since these patterns developed before language was functional, we need nonverbal means to learn more functional patterns.

The nonverbal creative process frees the *spirit* that was trapped in the earlier patterns of development. The creative arts are tools that can be used to treat those of us who come from substance-abusing environments.

The Creative Arts As Play And As Therapy

The creative arts address the healthy, playful, joyous, curious child living within. Movement and art use the arena of play to reinforce and enhance the healing process and to promote growth. We will look at how the two modalities of movement and art, as well as visualization, bodywork and affirmation, bridge and integrate the spontaneous child with the rational adult within the context of play.

Therapy and play are similar. Gregory Bateson suggests in his article, *The Message: This Is Play* (Josiah Macy, Jr., Foundation, 1956), that both are contexts of multi-level communication. Both imply a special combination of rationality and spontaneity. In play, the creative and cognitive live side by side. The combination within the same context, i.e. equating real with not-real, evokes the same emotional and cognitive patterns that govern perception.

Since the perception of his family is the cornerstone of how a child develops, it is the ability to change perception that will be crucial in the healing process and in creating more viable, dynamic ways of relating. When the creative and rational come together, a new integration of the self can emerge. The spontaneous, creative expressions of childhood are extended into the creative arts therapy session. The child, the playful aspect, is coaxed out and becomes the key element in transformation and integration of adult and child.

According to E. Erikson's *Childhood And Society* (Norton, 1963), play is the vehicle the child uses to work and rework the issues associated with the stages of his psychosocial development. In play, the child is continually acting on and interacting with the environment. Action and interaction are key tools for exploration and understanding.

Adult Abstractions And The Feeling Child

As adults, we tend to abstract out actions and involvements with the environment. We use words and descriptions as indicators of our understanding. However, descriptions are a step away from the ongoing experience. To the adult from a substance-abusing family, words and descriptions are not to be trusted. The initial primary experiences are, as mentioned, chaotic, lacking follow-through, judgmental, lacking intimacy. These experiences happened and were communicated first on preverbal and nonverbal levels. What is said and what is lived often contradict each other.

Visual representation and movement bring the adult's abstractions together with the child's immediacy and original feelings. Thoughts and feelings can be experienced as harmonious rather than dichotomous. To bring the adult and child back to the immediacy of his world is to bring the person back to living in the moment, which demands an involvement in life from the person's totality.

Art and movement are the bridge in bringing the feelings into consciousness and transmitting the internal spark of action. Allowing the inner feeling — the inner spark — to be continued into physical action and expressed in visual language makes clear our uniqueness before our adult selves can put a judgment on it. For example, during the movement warm-up, the group is asked to identify those parts that need stretching. They then move those parts in ways that feel comforting. Likewise, during the drawing warm-up, the group is encouraged to let their hands become the messengers of their inner feelings. The outward form can contain the richness of feelings in a single design or doodle. Identifying their internal needs and giving them an external form takes the "artists" back to their own internal spark.

Judgments Inhibit Expression

When judgments do not interfere with expression, we're able to see and reaffirm our uniqueness, which often gets lost in the thinking world. Exploring ourselves and our relationship to the world in symbolic terms allows freedom to play out all the parts that live in us. We can begin to incorporate and "make real" the aspects of ourselves that we wish to put into interaction with others. Sometimes a simple gesture can bring tears to our eyes because we experience the genuineness in the simplicity of the moment.

Initiating

The ability to initiate can be explored. A variety of interactions can be replayed several times during a session. Participants experiment with greetings, enhancing one another, staying together, transitions and endings through drawing and moving together. Since action, interaction and images are the primary ways of knowing the world, it makes sense to use those tools in the re-education and integration of adult and child.

In the family where substances were abused, we learned specific behaviors to protect harmony in the household. We learned how not to initiate because it might disrupt things — or how to initiate in a particular way to take care of everybody but ourselves.

With the creative arts we can play, practice and rehearse different ways of being with each other — expressions that are all okay. This allows us to see that the consequences of our behavior aren't always what we thought they would be. If we acted in a particular way in the family, that is not necessarily the way the world operates. We really can have some different behaviors; we can initiate when we wouldn't have before and experience some new responses from people. In this play space, this creative process, we learn a new repertoire of behaviors. We can see how this feels and how it affects others. Because it's play, we don't have to keep any response; we get to rehearse it. That's one of the exciting things about internal movement with ourselves. If we don't like something we have done, we can choose to do it another way.

Wise Inner Parent

The child is but one aspect of our very diverse selves; he or she is crucial in opening to new ways. There is also the very wise part of us. Sometimes we hear ourselves saying something very profound and pray that we are listening. This wisdom often comes from integrating some piece of information in a new way; or seeing an old hurt with new eyes; or seeing and feeling our parents with the compassion of a peer and not taking our own history so personally. As the compassion for our own inner child matures, the wise inner parent learns new ways of accepting, reinforcing and promoting new growth.

By choosing the path of our most expansive expressions, we can look to the creative process through the creative arts to fashion a playful, exciting road full of discovery and won-

derful surprises. The demons that show themselves on the
way are part of the quest and offer opportunities for growth.
The creative arts reinforce the life of each person that enters
the process of transformation.

Play is the context, the attitude through which the creative
process operates. Play has had bad PR. It is often seen as
something to do in our spare time. As adults, we are too busy
working, making a living, getting ahead, doing something
"worthwhile." Play is relegated to childhood.

Children, on the other hand, live the importance of play.
Play therapy is so effective with children in resolving issues
because it is their natural habitat. Why, as adults, do we forget
this basic truth?

Play Is Serious Business

In play, the rational and spontaneous live side by side; the
left and the right sides of the brain are activated to give us a
special combination that rises above the mundane with creative solutions. We can laugh at the child's musing, characters,
stories; they are so spontaneous, imaginative and alive. These
are the very qualities needed in the creative process of life.
We forget to stand on fertile ground in order to create; we stay
in black-and-white rational thinking, continuing to try to
figure life out when a child's musing could give us insights
we never dreamed of.

All the great thinkers knew the wonder of child's play.
Einstein fantasized himself riding a beam of light and from
that picture came the theory of relativity. He once said that he
was more dreamer than mathematician. The dream, head
play, is often the inspiration needed to spark a significant
manifestation. Then comes the business of discipline and
bringing the musing to life.

Creating a play space — a territory and time where everything is valuable — is serious business. In the play space,
there is no goal. Each moment is valued as a gift to explore.
Immersing ourselves in the moment, we get caught up with
the project, song, dance, poem, make-believe. There are no
value judgments in play — play just *is*. There is no good or

bad play. Play is a time to put on an old role and bring new life to a character; play is an old story with alternative endings; play is a new story — any order, any elements, any props. Play brings new meaning to life. If we discipline ourselves to play, new solutions will be forthcoming. Daring to play means facing all our old judgments: "You're wasting time . . . do something more important . . . you're not producing."

Allow the critic to be present in play but give him a hat and cane and make him the vaudevillian showman who announces the next guest. If we play with the critic, he may play too. Instead of getting caught up with criticism, lighten the situation and you've played with the critic.

Play is letting go of intense personal involvement with something and daring to laugh. How often have we heard, "Don't laugh, I'm serious." And yet, laughing is the very thing that would allow a different perspective. Play, humor, poetry, arts, music, dance are all multi-level communication involving both sides of the brain. It's in these activities that new perspective comes. Often, perspective is the very thing that needs changing.

We enter therapy because we need a new perspective. Our life view is limited, boring, stuck, dead. We don't consider play, laughter, art or dance as necessary first steps to new clarity. We enter therapy — serious business. Therapy shares the same ingredients as play and humor; the goal or focus is to change perspectives.

Perspectives change with laughter just as much as with tears. But we, as adults, look askance at levity when it comes to the business of our lives. The old "Saturday Night Live" group did a skit on "The Godfather In Group Therapy." Whenever Vito couldn't remember what he was talking about, the Valley Girl stewardess would look up from filing her nails and say: "You're blocking, Vito. I'm sure!" Group therapy was never the same. Laughter, when used appropriately, provides a lightness that changes our way of viewing a situation. Changing perspective provides a new frame of reference with new rules, new scenery, new ways of seeing. Effective therapy, play, dance, art, allow you intensity of emotion, clarity of thought and new options for living.

When we discipline ourselves to play, we guarantee quality living. Discipline — a commitment to the doing, knowing that the structure will take us beyond the constraints to new vistas — far from being frivolous activity, is daring to step out and say, "I deserve to live a joyously expressive full life."

See the self of you in action.
What you see in mind you can see as your objective form.
See yourself expressing creatively.
Give power to what you see yourself doing.
See spirit in perfect action.

Robert Bitzer

3

CREATIVE ARTS THERAPY

The notes in a magnificent musical composition remain the same regardless of the musician playing it. The difference in the impact and effect of the performance is in the musician's process. Some notes receive more emphasis, less accent, different timing. Some performances move us more deeply than others. Likewise in therapy, we, as clients and therapists, may have similar desires, objectives and goals. But, again, some therapists and clients seem more effective in their process of effecting change.

The vital difference is the belief and involvement in the process. As creative arts therapists, we share the same concerns as cognitive/verbal therapists: (1) What are the issues? (2) What are the communication patterns? (3) What are the alternatives toward healthier, more expansive ways of expression?

Equally important are the questions: (1) How will the issues be recognized? (2) How will the communication patterns be lived out differently? (3) How can healthier, more expansive ways of relating be expressed? (4) How can the attitude of play be rediscovered and lived as a mindset?

A dynamic process assures a quality life, one rich with integrity and aliveness, guaranteed for those willing to invest commitment. This process is multi-faceted.

In creative arts therapy, any interaction will have the ingredients of each person's style of relating. Therapist is as much educated by client as vice versa. Any interaction can be viewed as an art piece, through the eyes of the artist. Judgment is removed; description of what transpires replaces "right" and "wrong." If we view therapy as art, we coax out the process of relationship between artist (therapist/client) and media (movement, art, words, music, psychodrama, poetry).

Creative arts therapy demands the total person. A. D. Gordon, an existential philosopher, said: "If man is to rediscover spirituality, the proper balance between the two powers of the human soul — intellect and intuition — must be restored. A person realizes this totality by opening himself to the immediacy of the experience of life."

Therapy is an opening process. Individuals enter therapy with their unspoken definitions about how to be. They have lost or buried being "open to the immediacy of life." The creative arts are uncharted territory for most of us. As we enter into the process, we discover our rules, fears, ecstacies, trust, spontaneity. We find what is available, what is not, what is seen, what is hidden and what is yet to be discovered. We find out when we get frustrated, when we judge and when we can wait for what will emerge. This process demands that therapist and client not only learn *about* each other but *with* each other.

Likewise, it is not enough to read all the self-help books on human growth and development. Our lives are not integrated until our learning materializes through action. As Gordon says: "Spiritual life finds its consummation in the union of experience and act; man's knowledge of God is confirmed through dedicated action." Therefore, there can be no division between therapy and life. Man's relationship to a Higher

Power becomes embodied in his relationships to the individuals who people his world. These relationships have sometimes lost their immediacy and then therapy is only treatment plans, objectives and psychological jargon: "I'm in touch with . . . I hear you saying . . . I want to share." Somehow, the living relationship, honoring each other, helping a friend, confronting each other with all our parts, gets lost.

Courage, Dedication And Trust

We courageously and honestly identify our fear of a feeling or the unknown or the risk. Our tendency is to want to retreat from this kind of consciousness. As we identify our desire to retreat, we need to detach from it and recognize it for what it is, fear. We then affirm over and over again that it's okay to be afraid and go on with life. The fear does not have to stop us. As one author puts it, Life's emphasis is on commitment, the passionate involvement of man with his own mortal being . . . We, as human beings, possess knowledge not through reason alone but through body and blood, bones and bowels, through trust and anger, confusion, love and fear, through our passionate adhesion in faith to the *being* whom we can never intellectually know. This kind of knowledge we only have through living (from *Irrational Man* by William Barrett).

Start Where You Are

Where to start? Often, we don't validate our beginning feelings or situations. We want to jump to a resolution, judging our place as wrong, ineffective, inadequate. A prime directive for beginning therapists is, "Begin by respecting the client's place." The client is where he or she is by his beliefs and the way those beliefs have been reinforced by his environment. Identifying where we are in life and what works is as important as identifying what doesn't. Then we move into lifting judgments and generating options, whether we believe those options will work or not.

Next, we try on those options through moving, drawing, visualization — any medium that takes us into the altered state and has the ego step aside and take away the monitoring.

In the altered or free space the mind, body, spirit has an opportunity to wear the new options before our critic steps in and gives us the arguments, the infinite number of *but, but, buts.* In the creative space, a magical something happens that enables us to experience options in the present tense. The body benefits immediately because there is an attitudinal shift and the cells change if our attitude promotes health even for a second. Once our being experiences something that feels beneficial, it can never be completely comfortable in the old attitude again.

As we start from where we are, we can identify the form through which we are living. We can become conscious of the myths and roles we are assuming. Then comes commitment to change and the following guidelines:

- **Commitment:** a willingness, a desire for a more fulfilling, expressive life.
- **Discipline:** a structure and consistency that reinforces self-reflection, meditation, affirmation, self-expression.
- **Play:** a space and time that provides an infinite number of choices to be juxtaposed, mixed and matched; experimentation.
- **Breath:** techniques that increase awareness of breathing and how it alters when different feelings and thoughts come up; trusting breathing to support the process.
- **Risk:** trying on new behaviors in environments that require taking chances at the rate we can tolerate.
- **Maintaining the attitude:** surrounding ourselves with people who appreciate us and support a healthy, growth-oriented attitude; allowing the expression of all our feelings and frustrations but gently coaxing and reminding ourselves of those moments that work for us.
- **Stepping into a larger expression of self:** keeping the art projects or videotapes of movement that can be played again and again so we can acknowledge through all our senses that change is happening and we are not just kidding ourselves.
- **Listening to the language structure in cliches and conversation:** we minimize and put ourselves down by the

unconscious use of language. Such phrases as *not too bad, what a dummy I am, I could die for that, life is hard* are ways in which we keep ourselves stuck and pigeonholed. If we can listen to ourselves on the outside as well as the inside, we can begin to intervene and change those negative expressions to more descriptive and less judgmental ones.

* **Transitions:** bridges that help us move from one event to the next or one developmental stage to another; those clues that help us out of black-and-white living; turning clues and cues into immediate, purposeful action.

The creative urge lives and grows in the artist like a tree in the earth from which it gets its nourishment.
We would as well, therefore, think of the creative process as a living thing, implanted in the human psyche.

C. G. Jung

Creative Arts Therapy As Microcosm

Through the creative arts therapies, we can work on specific issues; e.g., impulse control (catching ourselves before we scratch out or paint over ourselves), follow-through on projects (finish a picture, complete a movement sequence), spontaneity (creating movement, art, poetry, without judging ourselves).

The creative arts allow us a place to be ourselves, acting out our worst fears and our highest aspirations. Moving or painting can allow us to practice letting go and provide the ACoA an opportunity to feel comfortable with seemingly being out of control. The creative arts evoke feelings about ourselves in relationships and give us a chance to safely express those feelings. We can check them out with others and see that we're all normal and wonderfully different. These experiences are safe rehearsals for changing our behavior in larger social contexts.

The interactions during creative arts therapy sessions provide the space for inconsistencies to be played out. Often, the way that a person experienced himself in early family life is not the way the world perceives him now. The immediate feedback within the creative interaction with others allows the adult child a chance to acknowledge the contradiction in his image and experience and fully express his present essence. The creative arts therapy session becomes a microcosm of the way the adult child handles himself in the larger world.

A man entered a mental hospital because he could no longer function on his job; he had lost a substantial amount of weight, was out of touch with reality and extremely depressed. One of the few things he could do was draw. He could do it by himself; he could keep himself away from external judgments and allow himself to just play. What emerged was an eagle with broken wings, the feathers blown off; he was very scraggly.

During the next six months, the eagle became stronger; the picture was in black and white but there was more color in the bird, more density in the wings and he got bigger. He then started to take flight in the pictures and he had a nest with eggs. By the end of the man's treatment, the eggs had hatched, the birds flown away and the eagle was ready to leave the nest. The man was discharged and returned to his high level job with a new confidence. The art experience allowed him to have a visual map of the psychological and behavioral changes he made in his return to effective and pleasurable functioning.

Nonverbal interactions with peers in the sessions flush out family dynamics. For example, lack of follow-through in a movement pattern or lack of ease in completing a self-satisfying picture speaks to the ACoA's difficulties in completing projects. Within the family context, there may have been little modeling for completing or consistency of an activity. Also, frenetic release of energy in the movement warm-up, along with high intensity scribbles in the drawings are the start of altering the nondirective aspect of the impulsive action. The impulsivity that thrust the ACoA into an unpredictable world with unpredictable consequences is the same spontaneity that can be used in entering a multi-faceted world that attracts exploration.

At the other end of the spectrum, the adult child's fear of moving or drawing is a statement about his fear of being judged. If something is visible, it can be deemed good or bad, the same judgments he experienced within the family. Being in a session with a variety of peers' visual and moving expressions affords the opportunity to experience a wide range of different expressions, all of which can be deemed acceptable. The movement and art session helps to move the adult child from a restrictive judgmental way of being to an exploratory, observant way of operating in the world. He learns there are gray areas or prisms of color with choices and options, all of which are a part of him, rather than the restrictive, black-and-white way in which he had been living.

The play space that emerges in the creative arts therapy session begins to spill over into life. There is less separation between work and play. What starts as spontaneous pictures and movement patterns reverberates into a more spontaneous involvement with life. Cultivating the seed of self-expression, turning down the volume on self-monitoring allows for a free space where anything is possible. The old patterns are allowed to dissolve and new patterns emerge, are enjoyed and integrated into life's creative process. Only when the ACoA can trust the play space, can new options arise. The ACoA comes to recognize that he has a vision and his vision is a vehicle to bring about change. To bring all his senses to that vision is to start to give expression to what is seen, felt, heard, tasted and smelled. To realize that his senses can be trusted to give viable information is to trust expressing or communicating directly. In communicating more directly, the adult child can experience his impact on and power in the world.

4

BODY SYMBOLOGY

The body and its movement patterns can be viewed as a map of one's life experience. It reflects the psyche as the voice expresses the song. We wear the experiences we've lived, the feelings we've expressed or negated and the beliefs we've developed. Our body's form has responded to early environmental messages and experiences and has compensated for maximum functioning. Form follows function and we carry the results unless we successfully release or transform the feelings and judgments held within the body.

ACoAs live by manipulating ideas and concepts. Living *in the head* gives the illusion of safety and control. Thinking and feeling in the same body seems overwhelming or impossible. The body feels like an enemy or an unknown spy. As ACoAs, we have the mistaken notion that the perfect idea will somehow transform a chaotic life into an orderly, sane, meaningful existence.

The Body As Database

The body is not recognized or experienced as a database for decision-making. Alcoholic parents are not consistent in

23

acknowledging or validating a child's sensory experiences. ACoAs learn to deny, distort, ignore and distrust their bodies. They tend to beat the body into submission, guess at what is pleasurable and hide their feelings in different body parts.

When an animal moves, it does not think about moving. It is involved in the here and now, moving. We feel, sense, see synchrony — natural grace, ease, unselfconscious movement. As part of the animal kingdom, we have the same ability to move with grace and ease. It is contacting that spontaneous, unmonitored natural center in us that *knows* in the same way an animal knows. When an animal moves into an environment, its body takes in the climate — safe, dangerous, threatening, confusing, easy.

We, as humans, have the same database as the animals but we also have concepts and ideas about experience. These concepts and ideas are associated with the original experience but are a step away. When we don't go back to the senses and original perceptions of the experience, we live in our heads and cut off the sensing mechanism that keeps us connected on the physical plane.

Our innate sense of reading our surroundings through our bodies has diminished. We numb, become unconscious of our bodily reactions to life and sort through ideas about our experience. Prescriptions on how to *be* abound. Our own intuitive knowing gets buried under opinions, stereotypes and judgments. We are our own worst enemies. We put ourselves down, diminish our efforts, belittle our progress.

When the process becomes a journey and not a rebellion, life begins to feel easier. There is a sense of curiosity, wonder, anticipation. We're not looking for the next battle as much as looking for the next fork or bend in the road. The feelings are still intact but the process doesn't feel like a life and death struggle. We begin to identify our defensiveness, our defense against our own natural grace in the body armor.

Until the judgments are silenced and body parts are reclaimed, we live crippled lives, our self-expression gagged. The judgments come from the many labels we have accepted from significant others including the media and famous people whom we deem attractive.

As long as we look at our body in comparison to someone else's body, we never see the form and capabilities that are available. When we look at ourselves in the mirror, we usually are being functional and don't *see* ourselves. Putting on make-up, combing our hair, straightening a tie gives us the opportunity to be functional with our bodies. When we change from being functional to *looking* at ourselves, our tendency is to judge what we see. We identify what we don't like and do not acknowledge what is attractive to us. If we followed the same procedure with our animals or plants, they would cower before us, bite us or wither and die. The same holds true for the criticisms with which we berate ourselves. We need to remember that there was a time when we took in images without judging, merely as information.

Old Baggage

Before words, there were images and sensory impressions. The infant absorbs an awareness of himself and of how to survive through a world of picture and tactile/kinesthetic impressions. Family dynamics are perceived and felt as images that are stored in the body and used as information on how to interact in the family. The need for nourishment and unconditional love that may have been an issue in the family tells the story in the adult child's protruding or concave, problematic stomach. Feeling responsible for family members at an early age shows itself in raised, held shoulders. Residual tensions in body parts contain the family secrets. There is a mistaken notion that holding on to the secrets keeps life safe. If there is no change, the adult child continues to play out the family myth. He carries old baggage into current situations.

Old baggage also includes fixed patterns of expression. In our families, there were particular body postures, facial patterns, gestures, use of energy, intensity in communication patterns. As we develop, certain body configurations were reinforced usually at the expense of others. When we exercised our movement options, we might have been met with:

*Walk like a lady . . . Don't use that tone of voice with me
. . . Wipe that expression off your face . . .* Children learn
very quickly what is a socially acceptable way of being and
certain movement configurations become unaccessible for
fear of being judged or punished.

Certain muscular patterns develop as the body develops.
Some muscle groups might be overdeveloped, others under-
developed, some constantly held. Armor develops as a protec-
tive mechanism against something perceived as threatening. A
chronic tension or holding pattern develops in the muscula-
ture. The holding pattern becomes a habit and remains unconscious until physical discomfort or disease is obvious.

The Body Never Forgets

The body is an incredible mechanism and has an astonish-
ing memory; it never forgets. Muscle groups compensate for
each other and unexpressed feelings as well as trauma are
stored in tissue, waiting for a time to come to the surface. We
may cognitively forget but the body doesn't. It's a storehouse
of information. It has innately stored and categorized self-
protection and repair information.

If the system senses danger, it immediately signals the organs of the body to prepare for the flight or fight reaction.
Without us having to think about sending direct orders, our
body chemistry changes to adapt. A greater portion of blood
goes to the central part of the body, the jaws prepare to show
teeth (a leftover affective animal response) and our muscles
tighten in preparation for action. These are all reactions that
take place many times a day in varying degrees without us
having to supervise every action. Often, we just need to get
out of the way so the body can do what it is designed to do.

In the process of re-owning our bodies and what is already
natural, we go through a meltdown, a letting go, an identifying
of "our way." We ban the rights and wrongs, begin to experience ourselves in terms of sensory data and describe our
experience. We quit rebelling against our way and begin to
identify our way.

We look at ourselves with appreciation rather than criticism. A changing body is preceded by a change of attitude. We look with the eyes of an artist rather than the eyes of a judge. To look with the eye of an artist means to look at form, shape, composition, proportion, movement and function as it relates to health. Before a shape can change, we have to have some idea of what is attractive to us, what pulls our eye and entices us to want to look. If we are overweight, tight, underweight, held and bound, all of these ways of being have served a purpose. We first have to appreciate the body as it is in the present moment.

For example, if we dislike our thighs and continue to have that thought every time we look at our thighs, we guarantee our overweight thighs a permanent place on our bodies. The rejection keeps the form locked in place. We have to somehow transform the rejection to appreciation. We can do this in a variety of ways. One is through affirmation. We might look at our thighs and say: I appreciate the weight for the protection it has given me; I no longer need or want the protection and I release you. The affirmation gives us an alternative perspective toward an overweight thigh. Berating a body part doesn't allow it to change. Accepting it, appreciating the function it has served and releasing it allows a change to occur.

The Body As Metaphor

The meltdown or release of the armor continues as we identify those body parts that are held tight, as well as those parts that are elastic, buoyant, available. We take inventory. The body is not only a thing in itself but also a metaphor for how we are in life. If we've created a fragile, timid body, our approach to life is one of caution and avoidance. Each body part as it relates to the total functioning of the body is also a metaphor for major life themes or lessons that we are living.

For example, in the oral stage of development, we experience our world through our mouth. When we are becoming more public in our lives and have to be more articulate, we tend toward a preoccupation with our words, our mouth, teeth, jaw and neck. We tend to use phrases that reinforce the preoccupation with the mouth such as, "I put my foot in my mouth . . . That was a mouthful . . . I stuck my neck out." Our lives fall into place as our bodies fall into alignment. Contained body parts impede the body in much the same way as an emotion or mental attitude blocks optimal functioning.

There are various ways to identify and release muscular armoring and input new, more flexible, effective movement options that reflect behavioral and attitudinal changes. The *Transformational Exercises* section of this book will offer some ways in which to begin the release of the armoring. Those releases, together with your reading and research and help from your local holistic health center and practitioners, will promote your further exploration in this area. (*Note:* In selecting a health practitioner, be certain that he or she can verbally process your ACoA issues during your physical release treatment session.)

Part of effectively connecting the mind, body, spirit is facilitating the health of the body and learning to light the cells with breath and vitality. In becoming adept at manifesting, we need to light our cells enough to generate opportunities and manifest with the same intensity as our minds.

We are vehicles through which a larger expression makes itself known. We are light receptacles which increase in intensity as our filament is able to sustain more light. When we experience ourselves as vehicles for the larger expression of a Higher Power and bring the small self in alignment with the larger expression, we transform the vehicle to become a perfect conductor of the light.

5

TRANSFORMATIONAL
EXERCISES

These transformational exercises are a marriage between the creative arts and Eric Erikson's eight stages of development. Before we look at the modalities of art, movement, body-work, visualization, affirmation, let's look at the foundation on which we use these modalities. Erikson's eight stages of development stress the inter-relationship of social psychological and biological factors acting upon man. He assigns specific psycho-social tasks to each stage, gives continuity to man's life and presents a well-rounded theory about man's development.

Erikson stresses epigenesis, e.g., each stage in the foundation for the next, and each crisis must be resolved in some way before the individual moves to the next stage. Each stage can be re-worked. Not only does Erikson stress the ego's ability to re-work a theme, but he even offers the medium through which the theme can be re-worked — play.

In this theory we see the child using "play" as a means of self-expression and "working ground" for finding viable solutions to life's problems. The Creative Arts serves the same function for adults when they play with the creative process to solve life's issues. Using the creative arts to explore the various themes of the different stages, the participant can experience new solutions and new ways of responding to life's problems.

In the group exercises, the creative arts provides the participants with alternatives for solving personal as well as social problems. The creative arts provides a tangible way of rehearsing resolution for social development. It provides immediate feedback on how each of us sees ourselves and how the group sees us.

Finally, Erikson's positive outlook toward a person's self-healing ability coupled with a healthy view concerning the role of frustration in development makes the total growth process "fun." He looks at frustration as an integral part of life. Thus development becomes an exciting challenge rather than something "we all must go through."

In performing these exercises, be gentle with yourself and follow the guidelines.

Honor your process.

- Allow the necessary time and space to explore without pressure of external or internal demands.
- Choose the same time each day so the expression of the unconscious knows it's going to be heard in a safe, predictable manner.
- Keep a journal.
- Create an environment that allows for your spontaneity by having available (1) a space private enough for you to move around in without feeling public, (2) a timer so you can let go of thinking about time, (3) journal books, art supplies, music tapes you like, records, player.

Painting is just another way of keeping a diary.

P. Picasso

Honor your limitations.

- If you hit a rough spot, write about it in your journal and take the journal to your personal support system, ACoA group or therapist.
- Be wise about who you share your private explorations with. Creativity, change and your internal self all need incubation time.

Honor your wisdom and desire to change.

- Modify any of these exercises to fit your personal needs.

Honor the spirit of participation.

- Observe, explore and cultivate a nonjudgmental spirit of play when you do these exercises.

We will offer body releases, art, movement, visualization exercises and affirmations that can be used by themselves or in combination. We will incorporate these modalities along with information about the body and its holding patterns. For the best results in using this information, remember that the more we fill our senses, the greater the intensity of the experience. The greatest transformation in healing and actualizing potential comes from incorporating the modalities of movement, art, visualization, body awareness and affirmation in everyday life. We will give a perspective on ways to approach each one of these tools.

Within each modality, we need to focus on:

Art

- the process itself
- the product, as it reflects unknown material or new material and conscious/unexplored material
- exploring and expressing (rehearsing) new behavior
- concretizing new ideas or dreams
- observing transformation
- circumventing the monitoring system

Only that day dawns of which we are aware.

H. D. Thoreau

Visualization

- practicing and rehearsing a new approach or comfort level
- changing negative imagery to positive imagery
- practicing seeing shades and colors rather than only black and white

No amount of skillful invention can replace the essential element of imagination.

Edward Hopper

In the dream state, Stephen LaBerge calls the ability to be conscious in our dreams and transform the images, lucid dreaming. *This process is one that can lead us to greater daily consciousness when we can allow the "monster" of the unfamiliar in us to come close enough for us to hear its message and let it lead us to new behavior.*

Body Work/Movement

- identifying old movement and holding patterns
- increasing and expanding movement, expressive repertoire
- increasing energy
- reducing stress
- promoting emotional and physical integration
- fuller expression of mind and spirit

True strength is delicate.

Louise Nevelson

Affirmation

- simple, powerful positive statements
- statements and beliefs about ourselves
- replacing negative beliefs
- serving as constant verbal reminders
- building new attitudes

We confront key issues as we move through the developmental stages. We will look at each issue, its corresponding "rite," where the body holds in relation to that issue as well as art, movement, visualization, affirmation.

Under each 'rite' we list a type of bodywork release that can be done alone. (Some readers may be experienced in working with a partner.) This is meant to be used as a sampling of the variety of psychophysical releases available. We encourage you to use the suggested technique or your own warm-up and release technique before venturing into the various experientials. This way your body will become a better vehicle for the expression of your psyche.

"To keep the body in good health is a duty . . .
otherwise we shall not be able to keep our
mind strong and clear."

Buddha

Issue: Trust

Being in life is transmitted to the infant through the holding and feeding patterns with its primary caretakers. This is the beginning of regularity and continuity in the mother-child relationship. Mutual regulation of frustration is essential to trust. Bodily experience provides the basis for psychological trust.

> *As the twig is bent so grows the tree.*
>
> Chinese proverb

Rite: To Be

Physical focus: overall strength and continuity, physical commitment to life, appearance of being grounded

Physical holding: fragile appearance or a look of holding on, neck tilted outward, legs thin and undefined

Physical release: Salute to the Sun — Hatha Yoga

These 12 positions and corresponding breathing patterns benefit the entire body by stretching the muscles and joints. They also stimulate the blood flow throughout the body and joints. In doing these exercises, allow yourself to relax and let go *into* the stretch and *go only as far as you comfortably can.*

1. Stand with feet together, hands folded in front of chest, quieted and attuned.
2. While inhaling, stretch your arms above your head and slightly arch your back and neck.
3. Exhale. Touch the floor with your fingers or your fingers and palms and bring your head to your knees.
4. Inhale. Bend your left knee and stretch your right leg back, touching your knee and toe to the ground. Look to the sky.
5. Holding your breath, extend your left leg back, parallel to your right leg and support yourself with your hands and toes.

6. Keeping your hands and feet in place, raise your hips to form a *V.*

7. Exhaling slowly, touch your knees, chest and chin to the floor.

8. Inhale while arching your neck and upper back towards the sun, allowing your hips and hands to support you. Exhale and move into a *V,* as in number 6, above.

9. Inhale, bringing your right leg up to your chest. Your hands remain on the floor. Raise your head toward the sun.

10. Exhale. Bring both legs between your hands, similar to number 3, above.

11. While inhaling, return to number 2.

12. Exhale and come back to where you started. You have attuned yourself through a cycle of positions.

Art: Inside/Outside Art Bag

Supplies needed: paper bag, magazines, paste or tape (stick glue is the best).

Individual or group exercise: Using pictures cut or torn from magazines, select pictures for the *inside* of the bag that represent your inner self at the present time, i.e., your thoughts, feelings, attitudes. For the *outside* of the bag, select pictures that represent the self that you show others. Paste the respective pictures on the inside and outside of the bag in an arrangement that seems to fit you right now. If you are in a group and you wish to talk abut the process or expression, select those pictures that you feel comfortable talking about. Give yourself permission to have secret places that you don't share with others.

Variation: The inside of the bag can represent how I see myself at the present time. The outside can represent ways of being that I want to grow into. The inside can represent what I choose to keep to myself. The outside can be what I choose to present to the world.

Note to the therapist: Allow at least 20 minutes for the construction of the bag, giving a 3-minute notice before the end. Discuss the *process* of making the bag. Listen for *descriptions* of the process rather than *judgments*. What kind of internal dialogue was taking place during the construction of the bag? If there were diversions away from the process, what were they, e.g. *I'm too tired . . . I'm not creative . . .* You might ask, "Do you want some of these pictures to be seen on both the inside and outside? Which pictures are easier to talk about? Are you judgmental about any of these pictures? How much privacy do you need with regard to these pictures?

Movement: Leading/Following Self-Awareness Exercise

Group exercise: The group is organized in pairs, with each pair having a *leader* and a *follower.* Partners face each other. The leader has eyes open and hands extended toward partner, palms up. Follower has eyes closed and hands, palms down, in partner's hands. Without talking, partner with eyes open leads partner with eyes closed around the room. Leading partner and following partner notice breathing patterns, where tension is held in each body, how changing direction and speed affects the following partner's trust level; how holding hands while rocking and breathing (without locomoting) increases relaxation and trust. Now change roles and repeat the exercise. Discuss with partner and as a group to hear a panorama of experience.

Variation: You can alter the exercise by having the leader (partner with eyes open) make visual contact with other leaders and find a way to exchange following partners. The following partners will have an opportunity to experience transition and find ways to get comfortable with a new leading partner's style. Allow time for each following partner to experience several leaders. Then, without talking, partners change roles. Discuss the experience after everyone has had an opportunity to be both leader and follower.

Note to the therapist: This variation often brings up issues of abandonment. It is helpful for the person experiencing these issues to sit with a partner with whom he or she feels safe, feel that person's hands and for both to breathe together and experience safety rather than abandonment.

Individual exercise: Stand with eyes closed and weight evenly distributed over both feet. Focus on your breathing, listening to sounds in the room and sensing how your body feels in a standing position. Stay long enough in this position to feel a sense of ease in your breathing. Then, moving in slow motion, change from a standing position to lying on your back. The object is to stay with every movement, noticing how your breathing changes, what body parts you depend upon to get from standing to lying on the floor. The focus is on the process, staying with every minute — not on the end goal of lying down.

Once you are lying down again, stay long enough to feel yourself and your breathing with a sense of ease. Notice how your feelings are similar to or different from the feelings you had while standing. Repeat the process, going from lying down to standing, moving in slow motion and staying with every move. Repeat the entire process until you feel a sense of *trust in yourself* in the process.

Visualization

Find a place where you can relax and not be interrupted. Decide on a certain amount of time that you can tolerate. This will change as you do visualization work.

Visualize, see, imagine yourself moving toward an open door with a sense of safety and quiet anticipation. You're moving into your perfect environment for rest and relaxation; rejuvenation; overall nurturing. Make any adjustments in the room that allow you to get more comfortable; adjust the temperature, light, air and surround the space with a color that seems most comforting right now. As you take in this room with all your senses, allow yourself to go to the perfect place to sit or recline. Feel your body give in to that place, being totally supported, allowing your muscles to relax. With each breath, your body goes deeper into relaxation, knowing that you're totally supported and safe from any intrusion. As your breath deepens, take in that color, which represents security and nourishment. Continuing to breathe that color more deeply into your system, allow the color to fill, wash and nourish your bones, muscles, organs, blood, giving special attention to areas of the body that seem more difficult to fill. Let that color continue to be generated by your breath into the room so that your breath creates a field of secure nourishment around you.

Feeling completed and whole, *"pay close attention to your physical signs of trust, safety and nourishment, so that when needed, you can generate the feeling of trust by recalling your physical cues."*

Begin to bring yourself back to reality by noticing what's supporting you and allowing yourself to move those parts of your body that need to be flexed or stretched. Open your eyes and take in the light in the room. Then do a total body stretch.

Affirmation

I am complete and whole within myself. Everything I need in life, I have within me here and now.

REFLECTIONS (Use this space to make any observations, notes to yourself, or reminders about your journey through the issue of Trust.)

Issue: Autonomy

This issue represents the inner struggle with doubt and shame. There is a need to prove one's own strength, which exists along with a reluctance to experiment with one's capabilities. There is conflict between retention and releasing, a need for self-control without loss of self-esteem, for new and different experiences to prove oneself. There is a need to explore within the limits that protect the child's physical safety.

Rite: To Need

Physical focus: relaxed chest and stomach; pelvis, stomach and chest in alignment

Physical holding: jaws locked, chest collapsed, stomach reaching and holding on, pelvis out

Physical Releases: Breathing Exercises

There are many varieties of breathing exercises. This one, *Rocking and Shaking,* is a stimulating exercise by Ilse Middendorf, the founder of Institute for Breath Therapy. Standing with feet approximately 10 inches apart and resting your weight on the balls of your feet, rock back and forth so your toes lift off the ground and back again. The weight can be alternated just on one foot and then the other.

Your shoulders, arms, hands and hips are loose and flowing with the movement. This will also cause a release in your back, neck and jaw.

Stop, sit and inhale. Your first breath will be like a deep sigh. Your breath will fill your torso. Then exhale slowly.

Continue to take three or four deep breaths into your belly, each time allowing the belly to return to a relaxed state.

Art: Self-Collage

Supplies needed: paper, posterboard (posterboard is sturdier and can hold more weighty objects) or journal, glue, markers or other paints, memorabilia, photos, pictures cut from magazines.

The self-collage is an expression of how you've helped yourself grow. When we see ourselves as the co-creators of our lives, we begin to recognize that we've attracted certain situations, activities and people in order to express more fully or to learn some new lessons. On whatever size paper or posterboard you prefer, begin to arrange in some satisfying manner those mementos, pictures and drawings representing those occurrences that have helped you grow. Remember that we need not judge experiences as good or bad but simply recall that they gave us an opportunity to change and may be an integral part of our becoming whole.

When you feel ready, glue the pictures on. Some articles (sea shells, a memento from your 3rd grade friend, the first record you ever purchased, etc.) may need to be attached in some creative manner, e.g. with string, safety pins, hooks.

Variations: It's strongly suggested that you create a self-collage for the way you want to develop yourself, what sorts of experiences you want to have or expressions you want to put into the universe. This becomes a visual reminder of your goals and serves as a daily affirmation for your direction. It should be placed where you can see it several times a day. This may also be where no one else views it since these may be goals you're striving to grow into and you may not be totally comfortable with sharing them at this time.

Since this is a collage that you're growing into, you will want to take an action on it every day. Baby steps are part of getting there. Small self-adhesive notes are great for jotting down one realistic action to be taken daily. When the action is complete, replace that note with another. This can be done for each picture or object on your self-collage.

Note to the therapist: There is a tendency to see only the negative experiences and to judge them as shameful events. Reminders are needed that what's important is what we *do* with the memories. Can we allow them to motivate us in a way that actualizes us or can we use them to help others?

Movement: Individual And Group

Group exercise: Form a circle and choose a piece of music that establishes a group rhythm. Encourage group members to make eye contact with each other while doing group rhythm. The group perpetuates the rhythm by bending and straightening knees (easy bounce) while clapping hands to the rhythm. Then, those members who feel comfortable in doing so, one at a time, go to the center of the circle and do any rhythm or movement that is different from the group rhythm.

Note to the therapist: The group needs to pay attention to the group rhythm as different people go to the center of the circle. How does the individual in the center affect the group rhythm? Vice versa? Does the group rhythm speed up, slow down, disintegrate? How do people in the center feel when they are doing their own thing? Do they feel immersed in their own movement? Embarrassed? Proud? Shy?

Variation: Have two or more individuals go to the center of the circle at the same time and each do their own thing, either playing off each other or in parallel play. What happens to the outside group rhythm when more than one person is inside the circle? Discuss each group member's perceptions of the exercise.

Individual exercise: Find a safe place and choose a piece of instrumental or synthesizer music with no words. Start in a sitting position. Focus on breathing and letting thoughts go. Then sequentially go through all the parts of the body, tensing a body part, then releasing it. As you focus on a body part, tense that part and allow all the other parts to relax. Notice how you use your breath in the tensing and the releasing.

After you have gone through the entire body tensing and releasing, take a few deep breaths and notice which body part asks for your attention. Allow the part to make itself known. Then begin to move that part *as if for the first time*, finding all the movement options for that part. Notice your breath through the whole process, finding ways to keep your breath constant and not hold it. After a body part has had its time to express, let it relax. Allow another part to emerge. Go through the entire body, feet and ankles, knees through feet, entire legs, pelvis, waist, chest, shoulders, arms, hands, neck and head. If you are comfortable, close your eyes and experience your whole self moving.

Motion is the nature of vibration. Every motion contains within itself a thought and feeling.

Hagrat Inayat Khan

Visualization: Meet The Guide

Visualize yourself moving through a field. You approach the far end of the field where there is a river. You swim across the river and stand at the foot of a mountain. As you climb the mountain, you enter plateaus of different colors, taking the colors into the cells of your body as you pass through each color. As you ascend one of the plateaus, you meet a Wise Message-Giver. You notice how your Message-Giver is presented. What age? What is the Message-Giver wearing? How does it feel? You formulate and ask a question, then receive a response. Thank the Message-Giver and yourself for this meeting and depart. Descend the plateaus until you are at the base of the mountain. Cross the river back to the other side.

Affirmation

I'm dynamically self-expressive. I have all the time, energy, wisdom and resources to direct and accomplish the aspirations of my life.

REFLECTIONS (Use this space to make any observations, notes to yourself, or reminders about your journey through the issue of Trust.)

Issue: Initiative

At issue here is your sense of guilt and the aim is to combat it, to become your own parent, balance your impulses with rationality and society's rules. It examines competitive drive and the mastery of locomotion.

Rite: To Be Supported In Independence

Physical focus: shoulders relaxed, feet stable and grounded

Physical holding: shoulders rising to the sky, chest high, hips pinched, "pushing off" with feet when walking

Physical Release: Self-Massage

A self-massage can be performed on any part of the body that needs a release of tension or increased flow of energy. For this rite, we are going to free our feet. If it is convenient, you can relax and bathe your feet in warm water. Begin by using both hands, wringing your foot from the toes to the ankle. Repeat. Starting at the toes, squeeze a few times back to the heel with both hands, fingers along the midsole. With one hand on your ankle, use the other hand to slowly and gently move your foot in both directions.

Support the top of your foot while making a fist and with your knuckles, press firmly into your heel, moving to the toes a half-inch at a time. Repeat.

With your thumb, push along the arch toward the toes; pinch with your forefinger and thumb along the outside of the foot. With your palm, gently and firmly pull your toes in and back, creating a stretch that you breathe into. Pull slightly on each toe and massage the top of your foot using small circles, with the thumb starting between the toes and going to the ankle. Finish with long, light strokes toward the ankle and a moment of holding the foot between your hands.

Art: Kingdom Of Efforts

Supplies needed: oil pastels, markers, paper, magazine pictures, glue.

This kingdom of your creation, drawn or in collage form, houses your interests, relationships, important thoughts, projects, roles and duties. The kingdom is your life at the present time. Each aspect has its own building, piece of land, significant tree . . . with its own size, shape, color, spatial relationship, representing its importance in terms of time spent there, priority, accessibility, amount of effort to get there, etc.

When you are satisfied that you have finished, observe your kingdom, taking in your appreciation for your efforts, the aspects you might want to change, time spent on particular activities and accessibility to significant people or ideas. Is there anything you forgot to include?

Allow yourself time to jot down your impressions, particularly any changes you wish to make.

Movement: Movement Initiation And Pass

Group exercise: Form a circle, pick a popular piece of music (words or instrumental) have the group do a simple bounce (bend knees and straighten) and clap to the music. When two people make eye contact, they quickly change places in the circle (going through the center of the circle) and resume the bounce and clap. If more than one couple is exchanging at the same time, say, "It's just like life; we'll find a way to get through without hurting each other." After the group feels comfortable with this exercise, have them make known their desire to exchange with someone by extending either hand toward the person with whom they want to exchange.

Variation: Along with eye contact and reaching out toward someone, you can create your own variations. Example: Make eye contact and, standing in your place in the circle, sink to a squat, then sprint as fast as you can to change places; or, make eye contact and *do-si-do* in the middle of the circle, then change places; or make eye contact and do a *high-five* in the middle of the circle. Practice extending toward other people with both hands to get a sense of which hand you usually extend toward people in making a connection.

Note to the therapist: Help participants identify the roles they played in the circle. Did they always initiate? Did someone extend toward them and they didn't see that person until the extender was right in front of them? Did they use their eyes *not* to connect? Did they hold their breath until the connection was made or while they were crossing through the middle of the circle? What observations did they make about themselves? About each other? When they were back in the circle, did they pick up the group bounce (which solidifies group support) or wait until they could make contact or be picked? What childhood memories did this exercise conjure up?

Individual exercise: Take a bicycle ride or a walk through new territory and go exploring by yourself or with a friend.

Try a new activity or take lessons in something you've been wanting to try or to do — swimming, scuba diving, dancing, tennis, golf.

Visualization: Special Gifts

See yourself walking on a road. You notice the road (country, city, highway etc.) and the texture (concrete, dirt, pebbles). Take in the surroundings — temperature, light, smells, tastes. As you walk, you begin to feel a buoyancy seep into the soles of your feet and move through your whole body. You feel quietly confident, available, with a sense of anticipation.

Off in the distance, approaching you, are two figures. As they move closer, you recognize each one. He or she may be someone or something that is familiar or unfamiliar. Each brings you a special gift. The first steps forward and extends the gift to you. You receive the gift, knowing it is given with love and wisdom. As you receive the gift, you take it in with all your senses, allowing its significance to speak to you. Give some time to this. The second figure steps forward and extends a gift to you. Again, receive it with all your senses and allow its meaning to be known. Take these gifts into your present environment, using their meaning to enhance your daily life. Thank both beings for their gifts. Depart, continuing in the direction you were moving until you feel ready to come home to your physical self.

Affirmation:

I am whole and complete in my being and doing. I enjoy experiencing new things by myself as well as with others.

REFLECTIONS (Use this space to make any observations, notes to yourself, or reminders about your journey through the issue of Trust.)

Issue: Industry

We will examine the ambivalence between producing and not producing, experimentation with the struggle to complete and the drive to avoid failure.

Rite: To Be Supported In Self-Assertion

Physical focus: shoulders, neck and head, with flexibility between them

Physical holding: full back, shoulders rolled, neck pulled in and thick

Physical Release: Acupressure

Relax in a sitting position. Cross your arms over your chest, resting your hands on opposite shoulders. Using gentle fingertip pressure, rest your second and third fingers on the highest part of your shoulder muscle (middle of trapezius). The weight of your arms hanging will be enough pressure. This point is frequently tender because of held tensions. Breathe deeply and allow yourself and your breath to relax into the sensation. You will gradually feel a melting of the hardness and may begin to feel a pulsation in 2 to 3 minutes.

Again, sitting — or lying down if that is more comfortable — place your thumbs just below the base of your skull (occipital bone) in the hollow between the two neck muscles. Relax your fingers over your head and allow the weight of your head to produce the gentle pressure. Again breathe and relax into the sensitive area until you feel a release and pulsing in 2 to 3 minutes.

Art: Adventure In A Lifetime

Supplies needed: four sheets of paper or four pages of your personal journal, oil pastels or markers — or pictures from magazines — and glue.

Title page one, *"Call To Adventure,"* page two, *"Night Sea Journey,"* page three, *"Fire/Theft,"* page four, *"Rescue/Resurrection."*

Recall an event or situation in your life that activated your growth, inspired a needed change or enlightened you in some way. These four pages are a journey through that adventure.

Although the specifics on your adventure are particular only to you, the process has the same components as myths throughout civilization. Joseph Campbell calls this the monomyth *The Hero With A Thousand Faces* (Meridian, 1956). In this respect it is a story of individual growth as well as a tale of human development.

Call To Adventure: On page one express in pictures, designs, doodles, etc. whatever motivated you to this event or inspired you to take action. Was this event something you were in by chance or something you consciously designed? How was this a process of finding yourself? Was it a feeling that moved you, or a knowing that action was necessary? Did you use your sensing or your intuition as a means of understanding this? Did this include other people? Did you anticipate it might change your relationship? What abilities or talents did this adventure require of you? What was your attitude about this undertaking?

Night Sea Journey: This page is the expression of your slaying of your monsters. Again, using pictures, images and designs, allow the battle to proceed. What did you confront? Was it outside of yourself, such as another person or the environment, or was the deterrent within yourself? What emotional state were you in and how did your inner dialogue help or hinder this process? What new thoughts or ideas emerged?

Fire Or Theft: This is the page of the Golden Box you've captured — or the fire you've won from the gods. What new concepts or illuminations have emerged? How has your behavior changed? What strengths and abilities did you gain from this battle? How do you see yourself now?

Rescue Or Resurrection: This is your expression of newness from the journey. You've allowed yourself to be transformed by that experience. The voyage empowered you in some way that was useful to others. What did this look like? How did the environment respond to you and what were your feelings about that? How did you verify and maintain your newness? Did that passage open new opportunities to you? How are you experiencing the result of that passage?

Note to the therapist: This experience will shed some light on which mode of functioning (thinking, feeling, intuiting, sensing) predominates with participants and which need facilitating.

The stages of this journey correspond to the four stages of creative thought: data collection, incubation, illumination and verification. They also correspond to the Breakout Heuristic cycle of growth therapy (Ernest Rossi, 1968): contentment (low tension), depression (introversion), breakout (high tension) and confusion (extroversion). There's great comfort in being able to observe our natural growth cycle as a process that's shared by all of nature. We can be encouraged to participate more fully in this transformation knowing that these cycles are a process of self-actualization.

> *Manifestation is not magic. It is a process of working with natural laws in order to translate energy from one level of reality to another.*
>
> David Spangler

Movement: Couple And Group Sculpting

This exercise allows participants to be active in their perceptions with significant others. Each can see that there are options in how to be in relationships with play with a variety of behaviors that elicit other feelings.

Couples: Partner *A* picks an important relationship in his present or past life. Partner *A* molds Partner *B's* body to a shape that symbolizes that person. Partner *A* then makes a shape for himself in that relationship. First, Partner *A* does the reality, e.g. how he is in relationship to that person in the present. Then, Partner *A* sculpts both Partner *B* and himself the way he would like it to be.

Group circle sculpture: One person from the circle goes into the center and shapes his body, expressing how he feels in the moment. The leader then asks the group: "What is being expressed? Does this person want support, distance, approval, touching?" One by one, each person in the circle enters into the center and creates a shape in response to the feeling shape they see. The last person to enter "names" the piece (sculpture) before he makes a shape. When the sculpture is complete, everyone returns to the original circle. Those people who want to initiate as the beginning person take a turn beginning the next sculpture.

Note to the therapist: Ask the initiator: Was the experience satisfying? Did the group feel too close, too far away? What did you communicate to the group? How did the group respond to the communication? Ask the group: What was your role support, disinterest, self-interest, non-involvement, discomfort? Where were you in the order that you entered: first, last, in between? Did you feel that you belonged? Were you an observer or an active participant?

Visualization: Animal

You are in a paradise garden. You wander through the plants, stopping to smell the fragrances, looking at the brilliant colors, feeling the lushness of this place. The journey through this garden is peaceful and safe. As you continue, you feel alive, present, exhilarated and curious. You feel an energy beside you. With a sense of calm, you identify this energy as an animal, taking in its rhythm, texture, size, colors, sounds and smells. You take on this animal's qualities or powers, to be in synchrony with it and to allow this animal to be your guide through pictures of a daily situation that presents itself. As you continue, allow this animal's qualities to give you a different perspective, to sniff out possible danger, the courage to venture into unknown territory and also serve as a protector. With your animal, replay the situation until there's a satisfying resolution. At the completion, ask your animal what you need to remember about this journey. Come back to your physical senses feeling rejuvenated and relaxed.

Affirmation:

I can be and do in the world without taking away from others. I am supported by the universe in completing all that I set out to do.

REFLECTIONS (Use this space to make any observations, notes to yourself, or reminders about your journey through the issue of Trust.)

Issue: Identity

This issue addresses rite of passage, integrating past and future; experimentation with roles and identity choices; desire for identification. It is concerned with the truth; with investment in causes, ideas and people; then with a rejection of that investment.

Rite: To Be Loved

Physical focus: pelvis in alignment under chest and head

Physical holding: chest enlarged, back straight with the pelvis holding out in back

Physical Release: Healing Touch

Go to your most comfortable, restful place, where you'll be free from interruptions. If you feel you could relax more fully by setting a time limit, do so. Lie on your back with eyes closed and begin by taking several long deep breaths into your belly.

Starting with your feet and progressing up your body, relax each body part, letting go of any tension that may be present. Rub your hands together several times until they feel warm and pliable. Place your right hand on your lower abdomen between your hips and your left hand across your heart. Situate your arms so they can rest comfortably without having to hold them up. Become aware of the heat in both your hands as though your body is opening to allow the heat to penetrate more deeply. Let your breath continue to be long and full as though each breath was charging and recycling the heat from your hands. Notice any thoughts, feelings, pictures that may arise and let them pass.

Trust that any changes you wish to make in yourself or your life will be imprinted more easily if your attitude is one of accepting life as a process. *Your task is merely to observe and be accepting and loving towards yourself.* As you progress, allow these feelings of love to fill your body. Without words or thoughts, continue to let them grow. When you feel completely filled, notice the physical sensations. Remind yourself that you can return to these feelings when you need to by recalling the physical sensations. Slowly return to the reality of your resting place, taking with you a fuller capacity to appreciate and love.

Art: Love Letter To The Self

Supplies needed: paper, marker.

Create some uninterrupted time and a peaceful atmosphere for yourself where you can bring to life in letter form your appreciation of your *self.* This is a time to bypass the *Judge* or *Critic* who can be so helpful at other times. The critic needs a rest from the job of being linear, evaluating, measuring and analyzing. This is a time to become your *Loving Friend* who sees your best parts, even those parts that aren't acknowledged by *you.* As the *Unconditional Lover,* you also honor the parts of yourself that are still rough because you understand this to be your path of development. Your *Friend* reminds you that you're loved as you — not necessarily because of the things you do.

It's suggested that you write with your non-dominant hand since it slows down the linear thought process and frequently accesses the less conscious material. As you begin, you may experience the *Judge* telling you, "It's not legible, this is a waste of time, writing so slowly, using too much paper, I have nothing to say . . ." Just notice the comments and come back to the feeling and observation of being your *Friend.*

Movement: Body Attitudes

Let the group walk in any direction at any pace. People are to call out different body attitudes. Each person tries on that attitude in the way they walk and relate to each other. Examples: uptight, hang loose, stiff upper lip, cool, sexy, stuck up, successful, loser, crazy, together, airhead, committed, iffy, dynamic, depressed, weary, elated. After the group experiences a variety of body attitudes, have them discuss the experience.

Note to the therapist: Which attitudes did the participants relate to? Which seemed uncomfortable? What attitudes did they wish they could feel more comfortable with? Ask each person to identify an attitude they would like to develop.

Couple exercises: Divide into groups of two. Each partner chooses an attitude that he or she would like to feel comfortable with. Have partner #1 assume the attitude while partner #2 watches; then partner #2 does a video playback through his body of partner #1's attitude, that is partner #2 mirrors partner #1's body attitude. As partner #1 watches the playback on partner #2 once again plays back the attitude on his body. Process the experience, then change roles.

Note to the therapist: What did people learn from the process? When the partners were doing the video playbacks, did the first partner feel criticized? How did the video playback feel? How did they refine or alter the attitude? What body parts had to be more or less involved? Was it easy or difficult? Did they like the adjustments? Try this exercise with a variety of partners. See if and how the process changes (if it does) when like sexes are together and when opposite sexes are together.

Visualization: Higher Self Taking Us To Physical Healing

You are in a dream landscape with colors and terrain that come easily to mind. You feel safe, relaxed, open, expectant because this is a land of your making. Feeling fully present, your *higher self* appears and takes you to a place where the waters come together. Take in the sounds, light, temperature, smells and movement.

Find a safe way to submerge yourself in the water, knowing that this is the pool of physical and spiritual healing. The waters are so bright and charged that they penetrate through the cells of your skin, gently cleansing and releasing the muscles across your chest. Your ribs feel flexible and strong. You feel the tissue under them becoming more vibrant and your breath feels more expansive. The tissue around your heart is feeling warm and open, allowing your heart to heal any painful experiences and memories. Take your time. The waters ease away all burdens from your shoulders, allowing your neck to feel more flexible and your throat resilient. Soothing, healing sensations wash across your face and head, pulling off any unnecessary tension. The warm waters sweep down your body, opening and elongating the muscles of your lower back and allowing the pelvis to release under you. Feel the cleansing of the water making your thigh muscles flexible, making your calves pliable and revitalizing your feet.

Take as much time as needed to feel revitalized by the waters in the presence of the *higher self.* Receive an affirmation from your *higher self.* Feeling thankful for the reunion, come back to your physical self.

Affirmation:

I love who I am and who I will become. I am committed to the ever-changing expression of who I am.

REFLECTIONS (Use this space to make any observations, notes to yourself, or reminders about your journey through the issue of Trust.)

Issue: Intimacy

This is a quest for kindred mates, for satisfying involvement in society, balancing and maintaining our own identity. It is a transition of focus from *me* to *we*.

Rite: To Love And Be Loved

Physical focus: physical alignment under the chest and head
Physical holding: chest enlarged, back straight with pelvis, holding out in back

Physical Release: Stretching

Stretching is important for keeping the body flexible and before we begin movement exercises.

Frequently our lower back will be our reminder of the challenges of this developmental level so we need extra attention on this area.

Lying comfortably on the floor with your knees bent slightly, slowly raise both knees toward your chest and hold. Gently assist the hold with your hands or arms laced around your legs. To begin, raise your legs only as far as it feels comfortable. Use your breath to release the small of your back into the floor. This is an act of sinking into and *allowing* the stretch to take place. It's not an exercise of doing or performing.

Continue raising slightly, stopping at intervals toward the chest so you can feel a deeper stretch in the small of your back down into your hips and buttocks.

Allow yourself some time. This can be done several times a day but particularly upon awakening and before sleeping.

Art: Nonverbal Drawing Together

Supplies: drawing paper, colored markers or pastels.

Couples exercise: Without talking about it, recall a previous conversation you had with someone — the first picture or situation that comes to mind. Notice whether you directed the conversation, initiated the opening or changed perspectives. Did you acknowledge, enhance or flush out the statement? If you're used to being the one who takes charge in situations and takes responsibility for others' feelings or good times, then allow yourself to be the partner who pays attention to the flavor of the situation and adds, continues, comments, embellishes. If you're one who prefers to meld with others, practice taking a comfortable lead.

Couples situate themselves on opposite sides of the paper. Each person chooses one color that's different than his partner's. This exercise is nonverbal so, without speaking, allow yourselves to create together on the page. When one partner is finished, he puts down the marker. When both are finished, discuss the use of space (balanced or uneven), who structured the picture, did you intertwine, draw at the same time or take turns, change the paper around for a different perspective? Check out with your partner any unknown or confusing messages. Would you have made any changes? How did you feel about the process and the finished creation?

Movement: Balance Exercises

Partner exercises: These exercises are designed to examine how partners physically set up a balance between finding their own support and supporting each other at the same time. Carry the metaphor into life.

Mutual support: Partners face each other, take each others' hands or wrists, lean back and find a balance while both partners are leaning at the same time. What parts of the body does each partner depend on to maintain his balance? While both partners are leaning away from each other and maintaining a balance, slowly come to a sitting position, supporting each other all the way down. Return to the standing position using support from both partners.

Stand back to back with your partner. Interlock arms, lean against each other and come to a sitting position. Remaining back to back, return to a standing position.

Note to the therapist: Mix the partners. People make assumptions about their partners according to their own body images: "He's too short — this won't work," or "I'm too heavy — she won't be able to support me." Encourage partners to talk with each other about what is needed to find a balance. How do they use themselves either by leverage or weighting different body parts, to find a balance? Ask participants who have an easy time with the exercises to help those who have a more difficult time. If one set of partners finds they can't manage the exercise, ask that another set of partners be used for additional support.

Circle: Have everyone stand in a circle and assume a solid base with feet shoulder-width apart. Find a comfortable way to hold on to each others' wrists. Then have everyone lean back, using their own legs as well as the group for support. Then, have circle return to their own sense of support. One at a time, each person leans back. Point out that the people on either side of the leaning person is their first line of support, but have "the first line of support" people practice a stance that allows the supporting person to get maximum support while the "supporter" is receiving maximum support from the circle. Each person gets a sense of being supported as well as the supporter. This exercise gives participants an opportunity to learn how to use themselves as well as the group for support.

Note to the therapist: Many people try to be the sole supporter for the leaning person so the arm connected to the leaning person is usually overworked, while the arm connected to the rest of the group looks like a "spaghetti" arm. We give the illusion of connecting while not using the connection to get support. Allow the electricity of the group to run through you; use the strength of the group to offer support to whoever is leaning. There should be a pull on the whole group, not just on the people on either side of the leaner. Continually look at how each person uses himself and the group.

Visualization: Heroes And Heroines

Allow yourself to relax with the anticipation of exciting re-
verie. As the relaxation deepens, a picture screen appears
before you. Images of heroes and heroines from your past
begin to appear. You are drawn to the attributes or qualities
that are particularly needed at this time. It might be the wisdom of Solomon, the altruism of Mother Teresa, the nurturance
of an earth mother or the humor of your favorite comic.

You see the figure and wear on your body the picture and
the feeling of the attributes. You become the integration of
the desired attributes, creating yourself as your new hero.
You, as the new hero, move from the screen to a future event.
As this new being, imagine the situation with as much clarity
and intensity as possible. Allow the hero to overcome difficulties, resolve issues, feel new possibilities, take action. When
you feel completed, return to your physical senses.

Affirmation:
I joyously express and receive love. I put out my highest
expression with everyone and everything I encounter.

REFLECTIONS (Use this space to make any observations, notes to yourself, or reminders about your journey through the issue of Trust.)

Issue: Generativity

This issue is about integrating love for significant others, for work, and ideas; moving toward unification of personal, creative and ideational life; desire to implement ideas and values for generations to follow, synthesizing all we know and feel.

Rite: To Be Productive And Receptive

Physical focus: left and right sides of body balanced, pelvis and head in alignment

Physical holding: one shoulder higher, one side of body more developed, pelvis behind body

Physical Release: Therapeutic Touch

This release uses a therapeutic touch and focuses on giving and receiving attention and energy to yourself. The body segments most involved with this issue of development are the navel area and head.

Lying in a comfortable position, rest your right hand across your navel and your left on the top of your head. You may want to prop your left elbow, to avoid having to hold it. Deepen and slow your breath while relaxing all your body parts. Focus your breath and attention on creating heat in both your hands.

Your mind will want to wander and you can pull it back to the sensation of warmth in your skin. Sometimes, seeing your hands as a particular color that represents warmth can encourage the process. Allow yourself as much time as is needed to feel the sensation. Seeing and feeling are major components of this work.

Start receiving from your solar plexus and head the charge that comes from your hands, as though a circuit of energy were being created. This exercise particularly challenges the ability to give and receive as both participant and observer. Allow yourself time to fully practice this.

*If the heart wanders or is distracted, bring it back to the point
quite gently . . . And even if you did nothing during
the whole of your hour but bring your heart back,
though it went away every time you brought
it back, your hour would be
very well employed.*

St. Francis de Sales

Art: Left-Right Dialogue

Supplies needed: oil pastels or markers, pen or pencil, paper or journal.

Select an aspect of your life that you're particularly focused on or that you wish to understand better. With your right hand, draw a picture of what that looks like to you at this time, using whatever style feels most comfortable for you. With your left hand allow a picture to emerge of what the situation *feels* like to you. Beware of our friend, the *Judge,* jumping in to save you from something that is foreign to you. This requires some time since we're unfamiliar with this process and because it's activating the right part of our brain, which is not concerned with time or linear thoughts. When you feel you are finished, observe any changes that may have occurred between the *seen* and *felt* pictures. Were there any surprises? What did you notice about the shift in your mood between right and left hand? How difficult was it to allow the untrained or unfamiliar to emerge?

Again using the right hand and the same aspect of your life, draw a picture of the way you would like that part to look. As you draw, allow yourself to see it as though it were in the present, as though you're participating in it the way you want it to be. Flush out as much detail as you can, such as time spent, people involved, energy expressed, places associated, what you look like . . . With your left hand this time, allow the feeling of your present active involvement in your ideal situation to flow from your body through you hand and express it on the paper. Allow as much of the physical feeling of the presence, joy, completeness, confidence and manifestation to be present in your body. What you're creating is not only the visual representation of your aspiration but the blueprint for your consciousness and training and nurturing for your body.

Giving and receiving are one in truth.

A Course in Miracles

Movement: Giving And Receiving

Couple exercise: Partner *A* is seated in a straight-back chair. Partner *B,* standing behind partner *A,* rests his hands on partner *A's* shoulders.

Directions to people standing:

1. Shake your hands and stretch. Take some deep breaths into your abdomen.
2. Rest your hands on your partner's shoulders.
3. Feel your feet firmly planted on the ground, open and not gripping.
4. Ankles are easy.
5. Knees are soft, not locked.
6. Thighs are relaxed.
7. Feel your pelvis under you and your back long.
8. Feel your shoulders melt. Feel the melting move into your upper arms, forearms, wrists and hands.
9. Allow the relaxation of your shoulders, arms and hands to release into your partner's shoulders: Do not hold your hands up and away from the shoulders. Let your hands melt into your partner's shoulders.
10. Feel the energy from the earth enter the soles of your feet, nourish and support your entire body, mind and spirit. Allow that total support to be communicated through your hands to your partner's shoulders.

Directions to people sitting:

1. Stretch your whole body through the soles of your feet, through your legs, pelvis, stomach, chest, back, shoulders, neck, arms, wrists and hands.
2. Focus on deepening your breath, the process of allowing and receiving, feeling the earth's energy come through your feet, which are flat and open on the floor, melting into the chair so all your body parts feel supported and nothing is held up or away from the chair.
3. Feel your partner's hands on your shoulders. As you feel the weight from your partner's hands increase on your

shoulders, surrender to the weight. Do not resist or hold your partner's hands up. Allow the weight to assist in the release of your neck and shoulders.

Note to the therapist: Talk each partner through the relaxation process, then have both partners bring their shoulders up toward their ears on inhalation and drop the shoulders on exhalation. Repeat 2 or 3 times. Have the partners sit, focus on their breathing and their partner's hands on their shoulders. Encourage both to relax and allow the breathing to deepen.

Ask the people standing to hold their partner's face in their mind's eye and send them warmth or healing or a positive affirmation or surround them in a color that comes to mind. Allow the picture or thought to be warmed by the heart and sent through the shoulders and hands to their partner. Have the seated partner notice the warmth and energy being communicated through and into their shoulders and have them send that healing energy to any parts of their being that need attention.

Change positions and repeat so each partner can experience giving and receiving. After each partner has experienced both positions, verbally process the exercise.

Visualization: Adult Child Integration

Take yourself into deep relaxation. In your mind's eye, see pictures you enjoy of children's faces. The children might be your own or related, from the past, children you have seen in picture books, television, movies. As you gaze into the children's faces, you see availability, curiosity, awe, joy, spontaneity. Use your breath to deepen and reflect those qualities in your own being.

As your relaxation deepens, you find yourself in a beautiful, lush park. You walk, taking in the sun as it streams through the trees; you smell the smells of the park, feel the breeze, look at the clear blue sky. You come to a playground where a little boy swings, a little girl races down the slide, two children play on a teeter-totter. Other childlike activities, familiar or new, are happening all over the park. You feel as much a part of this scene as the children, the grass, the sky. You find a park bench, sit down and feel joyous and receptive.

Off to the right is a gigantic grandfather tree with roots that go deep into the ground and branches that stretch high into the sky. You feel safe looking at this tree. At the base of the tree, something catches your eye. It's a child; it's you at whatever age the child presents itself.

The child approaches you and says, "Come and play with me. Come into my world." You go with the child into his world and play. Notice what part of your body is receptive to the child. Take some time. After a while the child says, "Come and sit with me. I have something to say to you. Sometimes, I want to tell you things that are important to me. I want you to take me with you into your day, find time for me."

As the adult, you listen to the child, taking what he says into your being. Bring to mind the wisdom of this child and its place in your daily life. Encircle the adult and child in a bubble of light. See the two merge into a new integration of both. Let your breath deepen the integration and notice where in your body the union of the two lives. When you feel ready, return to your physical body.

*Every child is a painter. The problem is
how to remain an artist once he grows up.*

P. Picasso

Affirmation:

I fully acknowledge my ability to give and receive with total abundance. I am public and private with my love and abilities and can know and feel their effects.

REFLECTIONS (Use this space to make any observations, notes to yourself, or reminders about your journey through the issue of Trust.)

Issue: Integrity

This issue is about understanding the life cycle, about a new and different love for one's parents; the awareness of mortality; refinding a sense of human identity and acceptance of the life cycle.

Rite: Mastery And Acceptance Of Wholeness

Physical focus: spinal column in alignment, head aligned with shoulders

Physical holding: back concave, head protruding

Physical Release: Immersion Into Water

The effect of hot water has been praised for centuries not just for cleansing and releasing toxins but for creating a natural state of relaxation and meditation.

Submerge yourself into very warm running or contained water. Allow your mind to relax and receive the quiet as your body opens to take in the heat and fluidity. It's been said that since we've spent nine months in the womb encased in warm water, the return to a similar state is the bridge between the invisible and visible worlds.

Concentration frees the mind for union.

Old Hindu Sutra

Art: Symbol, Mandala

Supplies needed: paper, markers or oil pastels, magazine pictures and glue.

Draw a large circle on your paper. At the top, or 12 o'clock position, write, SPIRIT. At the bottom (6 o'clock) write, BODY. The 3 o'clock spot is labeled, MIND and the 9 o'clock spot is EMOTIONS. Divide your paper so that each title has a segment of the mandala (circle).

This expression is concerned with seeing the balance in our lives. It's a visual representation of what areas are more important to us and which ones need attention in order to facilitate our wholeness. If we're spirit and lacking mind or body, we may be "no earthly good" and susceptible to physical accidents. If we are more mind and emotion but lacking in spirit, we may be more prone to addictions.

Within each segment, place your images (either draw in your own style or use magazine pictures) that signify your thoughts, feelings, activities, time spent with each aspect. What about that part of you is most important or is your ideal? What parts are an obstacle to make friends with or your lesson to learn with joy?

Note to the therapist: This may also be explored in the same manner with specific issues such as relationships, work dilemmas, money. We need to see not only the trouble spots but also the ideal in each area in order to better facilitate growth. Notice what elements in each segment may be similar or may be an access to a less developed part. For instance, a person may place a great deal of importance on his body and that may be the avenue to opening up the emotions through stress reduction techniques, body work, movement or movement meditations.

Painting is an attempt to come to terms with life.
There are as many solutions as there are human beings.

George Tooker

Movement: Self And Other Movement Extension

Group exercise: Form a circle and choose a piece of in-strumental synthesizer music. Have the people in the circle hold hands and rock from side to side, allowing the circle to find its own rhythm without anyone trying to control the rocking. Give the image: "We're standing in a pool of water. Our legs are slightly bent and go with the flowing of the water. Our hands are connected but we are not holding up anyone's hands." After there is a sense of synchrony and ease in the group, ask them to very slowly withdraw their hands and bring them to the heart, where they will rest.

Each person decides which hand to begin with. Then very slowly, using the breathing to support the movement and focusing on the hand, each person unfolds the hand and arm from the heart toward the center of the circle. As each ends the extension, allow the eyes to continue in the direction the hand is extending and notice the person at the end of the extension. Then, still sustaining and with the eyes still focused on the hand, allow the process of coming back to the heart. Repeat the process with the other hand; then repeat again with both hands.

Note to the therapist: After the group has completed the process, ask them once again to hold hands, close their eyes and rock. Ask: "What did you notice about your breathing and rocking as you extended? As you came back to yourself? Did you hold your breath? Did you stop rocking? When you looked at another person as you followed your extension, *if that person was not looking or extending to you, how did you feel?* Was there a difference in your feelings between your right and left hands? Was the going out or coming in more comfortable? Did you ever get comfortable with this exercise? Did you have any internal dialogue with this exercise and if so, what was it?"

After this exercise, play some light, easy, bouncy music and have people dance with each other in the center or do-si-do through the center, with only light connections.

Advanced variation: After the group has been together long enough to establish a strong bond, do the circle rock and extension exercise as described above. At the conclusion of that exercise, look at the faces of the people in the circle. Look with the eyes of an artist. What do those faces communicate? Allow yourself to look into each person and be looked into with no judgment, only acceptance. If the group is willing then, one at a time go into the center of the group and go from person to person looking into each person's eyes with the eyes of an artist or the eyes of a person who is taking in a wonderfully rich art gallery.

Note to the therapist: This is a very powerful exercise. Allow time to process or just be quiet with the experience. Have the participants write in their journals about the experience and also pay attention to any dreams after going through this exercise.

Visualization: Element-Blending

Go into deep relaxation. Begin this journey of integrating the elements of nature by taking yourself to a place in nature where you feel comfortable, refreshed, alive. Let your breath be your guide; it will support you always.

Breathe the environment into your body, feeling the moisture, taking in the colors and smells. Nature nourishes you as it nourishes the expressions of plants, flowers, minerals, animals. When you feel *at one* with your surroundings, see yourself move above and observe yourself as part of nature. From this perspective, take in the scene as part of a larger expression of nature, viewing animals, people, automobiles, city activity. Make any adjustments to feel comfortable with the ever-enlarging panorama and diversity of styles and rhythms. As part of your nature, expand your vision to include people of other countries with various styles, tempos and expressions.

Stay with this perspective until you feel a union of all the elements. Rise above this perspective and expand your awareness to include this planet as part of an ever-evolving universe. Breathe in the fullness of you as part of the expression that you behold. Breathe out a blessing for a more expansive coexistence and co-creation. Bring your attention back to your body when you feel completed.

Affirmation:

My Higher Power's opulence shines through me. I fully accept my life's expression as whole and complete.

REFLECTIONS (Use this space to make any observations, notes to yourself, or reminders about your journey through the issue of Trust.)

6

LIVING THE TRANSFORMATION

For any situation, project and desire in life, we must be clear about our intention. Dreaming, daring to want, isn't selfish or self-centered. Dreaming is setting up priorities in the future. The dream, the blueprint, has to be established and invested with our desires for our future in order for it to move in that direction. When we bring all our senses to the dream, we step into it and it becomes our reality. As soon as the picture is clear on all channels, through all the senses, we will live the physical reality of it.

That which has given me the idea fulfills itself.

Nancy Anderson

There are no mistakes; only self-regulating adjustments.
Living in the presence of the Greater Expression
is living in the center of our power.
Our life is our greatest act of creation and art form
and is a continuous, ever-evolving process.
Our gifts and talents are given from a Higher Source.
It is our right and responsibility in
co-creation to share them with the world.

BIBLIOGRAPHY

American Dance Therapy Association. 2000 Century Plaza, Columbia, Maryland 21044.

American Art Therapy Association. 505 E. Hawley, Mundelein, Illinois 60060.

Barrett, William. **Irrational Man.** Revised ed., New York: Grove Press, 1964.

Bateson, Gregory. "The Message, 'This Is Play' " in **Group Process: Transactions of the Second Conference**, pp. 145-242. Bertrum Schaffner (Ed.), 1956.

Black, Claudia. **It Will Never Happen To Me.** Newport Beach, CA: M.A.C. Printing and Publications, 1982.

Braheny, Mary and Halperin, Diane. "Non-Verbal Therapy . . . The meaning is in the medium" in *Focus on Family and Chemical Dependency,* Vol. 7, No. 2, March/April 1984. *U.S. Journal of Drug and Alcohol Dependence,* 1984.

Campbell, Joseph. **The Hero With A Thousand Faces.** New York: Meridian Books, 1956.

Cappacchione, Lucia. **The Creative Journal.** Athens, OH: Swallow Press, 1979.

Creative Thought. Published monthly by Religious Science International, a non-profit California Educational and Religious Corporation. 3130 5th Avenue, San Diego, CA 92103.

Erikson, Eric. **Childhood And Society.** New York: W. W. Norton, 1963.

LaBerge, Stephen. **Lucid Dreaming.** Los Angeles: J.P. Tarcher, 1985.

Landgarten, Helen B. **Clinical Art Therapy — A Comprehensive Guide.** NY: Brunner/Mazel, 1981.

Middendorf, Ilse. "About My Work." ("Aus Meiner Arbeit".) Paper read at Yoga Arbeitstagung, Willgen, 1972.

Rhyne, Janie. **The Gestalt Art Experience.** Belmont, CA: Wadsworth Publishing, 1973.

Rossi, Ernest Lawrence. "The Breakout Heuristic: A Phenomenology of Growth Therapy with College Students" in *Journal of Humanistic Psychology,* 1968.

Samuels, Mike, M.D. and Samuels, Nancy. **Seeing With The Mind's Eye.** NY: Random House, 1975.

Streiker, Lowell. **The Promise of Buber.** New York: J.B. Lippincott Co., 1969.

Helpful 12-Step Books from . . .
Health Communications

HEALING A BROKEN HEART:
12 Steps of Recovery for Adult Children
Kathleen W.

This useful 12-Step book is presently the number one resource for all
Adult Children support groups.

ISBN 0-932194-65-6 $7.95

12 STEPS TO SELF-PARENTING For Adult Children
Philip Oliver-Diaz and Patricia A. O'Gorman

This gentle 12-Step guide takes the reader from pain to healing and self-
parenting, from anger to forgiveness, and from fear and despair to
recovery.

ISBN 0-932194-68-0 $7.95

THE 12-STEP STORY BOOKLETS
Mary M. McKee

Each beautifully illustrated booklet deals with a step, using a story from
nature in parable form. The 12 booklets (one for each step) lead us to a
better understanding of ourselves and our recovery.

ISBN 1-55874-002-3 $8.95

WITH GENTLENESS, HUMOR AND LOVE:
A 12-Step Guide for Adult Children in Recovery
Kathleen W. and Jewell E.

Focusing on adult child issues such as reparenting the inner child, self-
esteem, intimacy and feelings, this well-organized workbook teaches
techniques and tools for the 12-step recovery programs.

ISBN 0-932194-77-X $7.95

GIFTS FOR PERSONAL GROWTH & RECOVERY
Wayne Kritsberg

A goldmine of positive techniques for recovery (affirmations, journal
writing, visualizations, guided meditations, etc.), this book is indispens-
able for those seeking personal growth.

ISBN 0-932194-60-5 $6.95

Enterprise Center, 3201 S.W. 15th Street,
Deerfield Beach, FL 33442
1-800-851-9100

**Health
Communications, Inc.**

Books from . . .
Health Communications

AFTER THE TEARS: Reclaiming The Personal Losses of Childhood
Jane Middelton-Moz and Lorie Dwinnel
Your lost childhood must be grieved in order for you to recapture your
self-worth and enjoyment of life. This book will show you how.
ISBN 0-932194-36-2   **$7.95**

HEALING YOUR SEXUAL SELF
Janet Woititz
How can you break through the aftermath of sexual abuse and enter into
healthy relationships? Survivors are shown how to recognize the problem
and deal effectively with it.
ISBN 1-55874-018-X   **$7.95**

RECOVERY FROM RESCUING
Jacqueline Castine
Effective psychological and spiritual principles teach you when to take
charge, when to let go, and how to break the cycle of guilt and fear that
keeps you in the responsibility trap. Mind-altering ideas and exercises will
guide you to a more carefree life.
ISBN 1-55874-016-3   **$7.95**

ADDICTIVE RELATIONSHIPS: Reclaiming Your Boundaries
Joy Miller
We have given ourselves away to spouse, lover, children, friends or
parents. By examining where we are, where we want to go and how to get
there, we can reclaim our personal boundaries and the true love of
ourselves.
ISBN 1-55874-003-1   **$7.95**

RECOVERY FROM CO-DEPENDENCY:
It's Never Too Late To Reclaim Your Childhood
Laurie Weiss, Jonathan B. Weiss
Having been brought up with life-repressing decisions, the adult child
recognizes something isn't working. This book shows how to change
decisions and live differently and fully.
ISBN 0-932194-85-0   **$9.95**

Enterprise Center, 3201 S.W. 15th Street,
Deerfield Beach, FL 33442
1-800-851-9100

**Health
Communications, Inc.**